VIA Folios 156

The Queen of Queens

THE QUEEN OF QUEENS

Poems by Jennifer Martelli

BORDIGHERA PRESS

The cover features "Pearls of Light" by Diana Torje.

Library of Congress Cataloging-in-Publication Data

Names: Martelli, Jennifer, author.
Title: The queen of queens / poems by Jennifer Martelli.
Description: New York : Bordighera Press, [2022] | Series: Via folios ; 156 | Summary: "In this tenacious collection of poems, the drugs, pop music, rocket crash, and Martelli's "queens"—from Geraldine Ferraro to Madonna, Nancy Pelosi to Molly Ringwald—embody the struggle with and resistance against gender oppression, political sexism, and ongoing threats to reproductive rights, while reminding us of the power of one strong woman"-- Provided by publisher.
Identifiers: LCCN 2021055597 | ISBN 9781599541808 (paperback)
Subjects: LCGFT: Poetry.
Classification: LCC PS3613.A77767 Q44 2022 | DDC 811/.6--dc23/eng/20211118
LC record available at https://lccn.loc.gov/2021055597

Printed with Ingram Lightning Source.

Published by
BORDIGHERA PRESS
John D. Calandra Italian American Institute
25 W. 43rd Street, 17th Floor
New York, NY 10036

VIA Folios 156
ISBN 978-1-59954-180-8

TABLE OF CONTENTS

for Geraldine Anne "Gerry" Ferraro
(August 26, 1935 – March 26, 2011)

. . . The proud boast of the Empire State,
the first lady of the Big Apple,
the Queen of Queens . . .

and for Vice President Kamala Devi Harris

What we don't know will hurt us,
but not yet.

DOROTHY BARRESI, "Chin Music"

Women wear the trauma of other creatures
around their necks, in an attempt to put
a pall on their own. . . . I looked into a
woman's tomb, its mother-of-pearl inlays.
A limp body looked back, into the gap
around my neck. I had no amulet, I had
no protection.

SALLY WEN MAO, "Nucleation"

Be as bold as the first man or woman
to eat an oyster.

SHIRLEY CHISHOLM

16 Reasons I Became a Gray Pearl

1. I grew tired of being a grain of irritation in the world's soft palate.

2. Thought I'd be a moon floating in a cloudy afternoon sky.

3. Being asexual, I craved bondage.

4. Craved four gold prongs to hold me in place on a band for the left ring finger.

5. Needed to backhand someone right on the mouth.

6. Felt silky, felt smooth.

7. Felt unsure so I committed to pescetarianism.

8. Bounced like an idea and got lost.

9. Was pried from my hinged jewel casket with a flat shucking knife.

10. Wanted to be shucked. Wanted to be shucked so bad.

11. Wanted sisters.

12. Wanted to be drilled and strung on a gold chain.

13. Wanted to *tink-tink* against another bead.

14. Wanted to hang around a woman's neck.

15. Wanted to taste her sweat.

16. Wanted to be dropped in a glass of red wine vinegar to see if I was pure enough to dissolve. I wanted to dissolve.

Shout, Shout

—Tears for Fears

These are the things I can do without: one day of prayer, 50 pearl beads each
an *Ave Maria*, 20 cigarettes, a milk heart floating on my coffee.

I shouldn't have to jump for joy on the red brick walk
past the *Friendship* docked in Salem Harbor. But I do.

At the Tarot shop across the street, Doug the reader turned over the Star:
trauma has passed during the night; pain is now a pleasant itch.

The *Friendship* is docked right there, on the high water in Salem.
Who wouldn't want to break a heart? Who wouldn't want that power?

Also, I can do without: a cricket's wings, my father's Ray-Bans,
a sea dollar, a sea star, a base line, a spondee, a spondee.

from *Jezebel*: "Map: Six Decades of the Most Popular Name for Girls, State by State"

Jezebel's map of girl names was green/gray for the 60s: each state filled
    with Marys
and Lisas until Jennifer Cavilleri, the working-class Italian Cliffy
    in *Love Story* who died
of leukemia in the 1970 movie, birthed a new generation of Jennifers.
    As she died,
she didn't expect much because *love means never having to say you're sorry.*

~

On *Romper Room*, another Jennifer emerged from Miss Jean's Magic
    Mirror.
I sat cross-legged and too close to the black and white TV, the one
    with tin-foiled rabbit ears
in the little den off the pink kitchen where my mother smoked. I
    thought I was the only Jennifer.
I was the only Jennifer I knew, which is why *I fell off the round and
    turning world.*

~

As a meta poem, this would be like a shattered mirror. Here is Miss Jean
saying, *And I see Jennifer.* There's Donovan singing *Jennifer Juniper.*
This is my sixth-grade project on leukemia. This is where I lived:
among lawn statues of Mary, Queen of the Universe.

Jennifer began to eat the Marys, the Lisas off the map of green and
     gray state names—
Jennifer flooded the map with bright blood red. The whole country
     on the *Jezebel* map red,
red as a Republican electorate. I watched this time-lapse over and over:
and it's like a bad election night, each state filled up completely red,
     even Massachusetts, even there, and Jennifer ruled for 15 years.

The National Post called this era "The Jennifer Epidemic," and it was
     feverish,
flushed, genetic and bell-curved. But in 1984, the Jennifer fever
     broke, the blood
bloom stanched. Jennifer retreated from the nation's cool white forehead, left
a neutral memory: curled like a nail, a hook, like the letter J my
     mother fell in love with.

So, if you insist I submit this anonymously, I'd have to erase or redact
     each Jennifer
replace her with _____ or ~~Jennifer~~. I'd want
not a hum in your mind, but an expelled breath so when you read
     this you would
asphyxiate and hyperventilate quietly, see stars before your eyes.

Why I Began Writing About Vice Presidential Candidate, Geraldine Ferraro

Behind Commonwealth Avenue, next to the old domed temple
they turned into an observatory, the theater

premiered *Flashdance.* After that, no one
wore a sweatshirt without the neckhole torn to the shoulder knobs

like Jennifer Beals who unhooked her bra, pulled it from the sleeve
without ever breaking eye contact.

Someone smarter than I must know how many times
I've orbited over three decades. Everything then

is happening again: back in the '80s, a rich man
raped his first wife and now I have to look at his face every day.

Last night, I streamed Jennifer Beals on all
my devices. How I love her every move. Of course,

she was a welder during the daytime. I took
the one freshman in my dorm who looked like the steel mill owner
up to my single room. What I mean is,

when my joints pop, when I'm like
a maniac, maniac on the floor,

ghosts come. I don't come
to anything in quiet. Maybe it was there,

on the cold linoleum, maybe against the cinderblock bricks. Maybe
it was in the towers with this stupid boy on top of me
that I was hopeful I could conjure

anybody or thing I wanted.

Oracular

In the year of Ferraro, I loved my drugs, my runic-ludes,

      loved to dance under those mirror balls,

thought I was beautiful, thought I was heard.

I carried a skinny mirror back then—

      wet my gums, shaped my brows. Saw the sky,

saw an 8-ball moon. I saw The Cure.

The First Lady loved astrology, loved Chanel.

      She loved her little body all wrapped in red—

a real picker-upper, she said. The cut-glass mirror beads

on her de la Renta sheath refracted light, all crystal

      white. She read the stars. She loved

her husband's moons, his metal pig, his licorice beans. On a mirror

I wrote my name in powder, deep-

      bellied beneath a night club floor. I heard

half-disco/half-punk feet dance over me, beneath the mirror ball.

Could you hear me?

    Whole nights and into the next spent dancing—

we loved our drugs, we loved our ludes, we tossed back

    the luminous runes:

      you are heard, they said: they said, *you are beautiful.*

Questions to the Electorate

*The Catholic Church is [not] monolithic
in its teachings on abortion,* Geraldine
Ferraro, 1984

Is a man a monolith?
Can you decorate a monolith with sprigs of nutmeg, rue,
          pennyroyal, a garden of abortifacients?
Can you grow savin, squills, ergot of rye around the monolith?
Can you dig down far enough so the roots will embed?

Can I rule as a monolith?
Can I rule as a woman who's had not one but two,
two abortions? And still is not sad?
Can I rule as a woman who is not sad at all?

Can we drape the monolith with pearls: chunky fake gems?
Can we polish its flat dark marble surface until it shines
like the tombstones in the Italian cemetery? Will you circle
          the monolith?
Will you join hands with me and dance and dance and dance?.

Star Sign of the Moscone Center, July 19, 1984

was Cancer with a waning moon

was a salt-water teardrop sign

was least lucky in love

held sway over the head, the teeth, the tongue

was a Leopard Lady Crab from Long Island Sound

sidled up to the stage and sang like Cyndi Lauper

I wanna be the one to walk in the sun—

polished her purple pincers until they shone under the hot lights

tasted the salt dripping off of Geraldine Ferraro's pearls

was extra mean and wanted to bite

was molted and re-homed herself

was in America

wondered where the sun would be placed

wondered when she would shine.

—after Joan Quigley, Reagan White House Astrologer

Strega

Long ago, when I needed to be numb,

I offered my loves clear broth
in mercury glass bowls so
they never knew what they held and I
could read their emotions in degrees
Fahrenheit.

Now I bring myself to everyplace I go,
sure that my body is 60% salt water,
40% deserted island. A woman
waits in the field that grows
along my diaphragm. She holds a yellow
snake with pearly pink eyes. I can hear the blades
of grass groan. Someday, before I

end, I'll leave that island, sail to the colony
in my belly, or maybe swim to the kidney-
shaped grotto. And I'll own what's there.
Understand, that if you cut me
in half, one of my sisters will grow. That

sometimes I am my children, and those times
are the most painful.

Relinquishing

For months now I've refused three types of flesh: from a cow, a pig,
a fowl.

I'm not pure, though. I can't resist cheese in its clotted shades: creamy
knobbed

and knotted mozzarella, bone chévre, veined bleu.

For X-mas, G. mailed me a tin of struffoli: small balls of fried dough
drenched in honey,

sprinkled with candy beads. Sticky gold drops on the tin lid.

The bees in the comb that made that honey, humped, and were smoked
out of their hive: they

loved their queen left all baffled and alone. Someday

my kids may write about me—not a poem, but maybe a list of all
the hurtful

seedlings I planted like radium in their glands. Maybe

they will remember some love too, though I was mostly afraid. G.'s
cancer leaps

throughout her body. When I call to thank her, we talk about
turmeric.

I ask her, as a vegan, would she wear pearls? The oyster, pried open
for its hard

comforting spit, looks clitoral: the salty, faceless meat.

Tongue Root

I have always lived by the ocean. When I was a child, I built my altar at low-tide on Revere Beach. I made a pentacle with:

1. a small, suede fringe pouch I stole from one sister with my other sister's doll tucked inside
2. the blue plastic pirate sword I pulled from the heart of a Maraschino cherry
3. grandpa's skeleton key I found dangling from a hook on grandma's stove
4. from my mother's pocket, the book of matches from The General Edward's Inn
5. my father's tarnished brass tie pin with an embossed tiny White House.

What I conjured then, I live with now. I conjured women nobody heard.

I asked my friend, who has the same name as I, *Do people think I'm not so bright? No one thinks that,* she said, *but you have a strong accent.*

Long ago, everybody I knew had last names like mine, all ending with a long, rounded vowel. Vowels have heft. Like planets orbiting, they are frictionless, compulsive, and smooth. The vowel is the nucleus of a word. Everything—all sound—depends on the position of the tongue root for articulation, for movement.

Maybe people hear me and think I've never left this place. There are whole sounds I elide, delete, and erase. There are whole periods of time, too. There are people. What I mean is no one taught me to: pronounce a whole phoneme, to roll my tongue, to open the glottis, to think that ghosts won't appear when I speak.

Agrodolce

The whole world skewed on its iron axis.
I ate a lemon from the groves on the coast of Campania: citrus so big
I cupped it like a heart in my two lined palms, sunk my teeth into
    sweet pulp.

Can you feel the juice as I say this?
Can you feel it in your jaw's hinges, in your ears?

Deep inside those warm canals, there's an anvil forging sounds—
meanings hammered out. Do you wonder what people are saying
    about you?
Do you wonder if people say anything at all?

At some point, we all disappear. I had the strega read
my right-hand lifeline: it crossed my thumb mound and circled my wrist
like a healing wound. This was a plot as well. I asked her to read
what was on my left. *You are unable to avoid what you wish to.*

I swallowed the soft bodies of oysters that same oracular night—
their shells told a story too, a landscape. Their bodies tasted
like a blue-green ocean, like a woman taken whole into my belly.

Fugue

I choreograph the deep distance between me and the shadows.
Twice in my life ghost-women manifested in my hinged joints:
my elbow, the first knuckle of my left pointer finger, my jaw.
They manifested in the cabinet where I keep chipped china,

in the tortoiseshell cup I stole from my father's bureau. I didn't know
how fragile everything was. Something like glass cracks, then silence,
then I stop under an overcast sky, heavy and low
as a whale's belly full of gray pearls, the shadow of the gulls.

Pleasant Street's blacktop split after the quick freeze.
It is all but deserted. I wear my camel-colored coat,
walk down to the post office, past the purple croci
that broke through too soon, fooled by an early thaw,

past the shop that repairs glass and displays panes and mirrors
in its storefront window: the man inside measures and cuts,
smokes and waves to me. Storm door frames lean on the façade.
The gulls are bold and hungry now, flock blocks from the beach.

Grey Figs and Leaves, by Wedgwood

My mother's china was bone-white, barely used, and rimmed with
  14-karat gold.

Nobody wanted it after she died deep into that awful summer. The bowls

were too shallow, could barely hold one ladleful of the aglio olio that only

my uncle was allowed to make each Christmas Eve. The olive oil rose

in fat round shapes, made a slick layer on the hot broth, above the angel

hair, around the single anchovy: its salty-thick ocean taste lasting too long.

My great-aunt, the strega, would read our futures: how the oil refused
  to sink,

how it refused to join. How the oil could look like a monster's egg
  or the lost

green beryl that fell from my mother's ring.

Sometimes, I forget what is memory and what is wished for.

Would my mother be with me for all time. Would I keep her china
  with the wreath

of grey figs and leaves with metal paint that could explode. What of
  her ring.

I Sleep in the Daytime

"Life During Wartime," Talking Heads

Yesterday, in my half-lucid dream, this: two pearls
just outside the bedroom window. I know they were
   my parents.

I'd watched a movie deep into that night
when time stopped mattering: all the angels
in heaven were sent by God to destroy us—

they came down the road, the sky
was a dark ocean. (Believe me, the women

who've come to me in my poems hold
my parents deep within their bones—and now
I have to keep still in my sadness).

The coastline where I live is shaped like hooks
for miles. I walked three beaches at low tide.

Washed-up rocks made a moonscape: some white
and speckled like the eggs of a great reptile,
some rusted tigers' eyes, some smooth, iridescent.

He is My Man. He is My Tomato.

Why haven't you taken your husband's name?

What is a love apple?

Has he paid his taxes?

What fruit is not native to Italy?

Who is Luca Brasi? John Gotti? Vinnie Barbarino?

What is a Beefsteak, a San
Marzano, a Black Krim?

Does your husband also support the murder of babies?

What fruit has meat and skin and
bleeds?

Has your husband ever killed a man?
Rented a room to a pornographer?

What would you like on your
burger?
What fruit's bitterness is neutralized
with sugar?

What of your father? What of your husband's father,
how did he die?

What fruit was too cold? Too wet
for the Italians to swallow raw?

What does your God look like? Your priest? Your Pope?

What is an Early Girl, a Tigerella,
Three Sisters?

Vice Presidential Acceptance Speech by Congresswoman Geraldine Ferraro, July 19, 1984

Ladies and gentlemen: My name is

(~~not~~)

that

American

woman

(~~not~~)   our own

sister

daughter   mother (~~not~~)

you.

Prognostication

I do not gaze into crystal balls, Joan
Quigley, Nancy Reagan's astrologer

In the '80s I experienced five types of hunger, but never the one that
ended in nourishment. There was the hunger for love. The hunger
for freedom from bondage of self. The hunger for cock. The hunger
for full moons. The hunger to know.

A strega lived on my street. She would take a gold-rimmed white plate,
pour a drop of green olive oil in the middle of water, grind pepper, and
read the future. If the pepper flakes made a circle, an argument was in
the offing; if they scattered like the stars, recovery was possible. The
oil floated on the water: sometimes a large moon circle, sometimes
pearlescent beads.

I would go upstairs to my friend T.'s bedroom, in the Cape Cod-style
house she lived in with her father and her brother: her room, tucked
under the dormer. Next to her French Provincial bed, there was a little
door we had to bend down to enter. A long attic spanned the length
of her house, to her brother's room. It was their umbilical cord, their
leash, their string phone.

And the phones had touch-tone buttons, faster than the old dials
you had to drag back to zero. We hovered our hands over the square
buttons, asked about each boy who broke us: *but do you think he'll
call?* Sometimes, the phone rang. Back then, we could call to get the
weather forecast and the exact time.

One night, we dressed for a costume party at a club. T. had saved her
mother's silk and chiffon scarves. We draped them over our faces and
around our waists. Some scarves had unraveled fringe, one had tiny
seed pearls. We wanted to see the future.

Then, J. came through the long attic with packets of cocaine he weighed on a chemist's scale and folded into tiny envelopes. We needed a perfect place to inhale it through the gold-plated straw: not off the floor, not off the glass covering the photo of her mother, not off her first communion bible. Maybe the tender webbing between our fingers and thumbs. We found her round cracked make-up mirror in a black satin Gucci clutch with a pearl clasp.

I pleaded with so many boys not to leave me. One boy's shoulders swayed like a lever on a fulcrum as he walked away. His white shirt glowed in the moonlight. In a nightmare, I couldn't make my fingers work the phone to call him. I couldn't speak loud enough for him to hear me.

In the Year of Ferraro

*To not see your personage reflected
in politics is a pain,* Marie Wilson,
former president, Ms. Foundation
for Women

I had a pair of Vuarnet sunglasses, rims as red
as *come here, come.* I sold them for one gram
of cocaine in a little white envelope.
I had five more years of relinquishing.

I couldn't see that then.

Friends wore Ray-Bans like Tom Cruise
in that movie where he danced in his boxers and white shirt.
Remember how he broke his mother's crystal egg and she
saw the crack when she turned it this way and then that to the light?

Think of how information travels. So much enters through the eye.

The dark pupil dilates and constricts, pulls tight and shut:
nothing that goes in can leave or ever go back.

Mal'Occhio

Last night the new moon bloomed
the green leaves

on my backyard maple,
urged the tiny glow worms

down from their silk threads
onto the oxidized

eaves of the feeders.
The vernal pool dug out

from the broken sidewalk
had an airtight seal

of pollen: nothing could survive.
I'd gone to sleep

envious. I woke
to the news: a brutal

man hanging from a cotton noose
in his cell. None of this

was in my mind. The birds
circling since before the day broke:

even they were starved.

Toxic Shock Duplex

Last night my ghost period came to visit.
      She dragged the white string from the sky's cervix.

What I hold onto will drag me for certain.
      My fearful life is knotted like a pearly helix.

I've lived my life in fear of not existing.
      I found an old box of Easy Glide Pearl Tampax.

The glide was easy, but the white bloomed toxic.
      Long ago, I found the cure for disappearing.

To not disappear and to be found almost killed me.
      Today I walked under the pink magnolia trees.

But the pink lasts under a day on the old magnolia trees—
      the leaves fall pearly and slick to the cracked sidewalk.

I'm shocked when people leave or when they walk back.
      The ghost meant only to last a night. Period.

My Father Was an Italian Man. So Are My Husband and My Son.

—Geraldine Ferraro

Sometimes, when my stiff joints pop, women appear and want to talk to me.

No matter how carefully I move, these women want to use their tongues.

We all know that the dead can't speak, but some can shake rice in a tin sieve.

A poet told me the first tambourine was formed in Italian groves

where women danced while cleaning rice and later, where women conjured ghosts.

I was ashamed to tell them I swapped my father's name for my husband's:

the vowels so round at the end, they slipped into my smooth white sockets.

No matter how far back I searched, the names were fathers' names— thick as guns.

If I owned a gun, it would have a cool, ghost-white mother-of-pearl grip

and an exposed silver-toned barrel, silver back strap, slide, and hammer.

Its sound would sound more like air sucked out from small pink lungs, or finger snaps.

No matter how far back I traveled—Avellino, Salerno, Rome—

all I found was a man's silver axe, his hammer, a boy, a blacksmith.

No matter how I move now, women pop out of me. They sound like guns.

Ghost Hunters

The hunters with their moon-green eyes
and camera helmets catch ghosts on film—

I watch the videos in our hotel room on Via de Martelli
off the Piazza del Duomo. Everything

in this province had my husband's name.
The early evening downpour caught us

along the Arno where a small
terra cotta shop dangled over the river, split

the rain into two sheets. I watched it fall
while I ate cold sweet lemon cream from a bone

china bowl with the Cathedral of St. Mary of the Flower fired
onto the enamel: once red, now soft

pink. The ghosts on television open doors
slowly, inch by inch. Their shadow arms

too weak to do much more. They can't even talk
or comb their hair, though sometimes they shine

like new moths or pearls. Back home, it isn't dark,
it isn't the time it is here, in Florence. I've lived

through a whole day my friends have not.
I can barely make out the translations for *ghost* low

on the screen: *fantasma, spettro, ombra:*
wraith and spirit and obscurity.

Cisoria

I've been home for weeks, slicing cotton into strips
for masks: *the terrible wind tries its breathing.*
I've been searching for loose-weave cloth and shears.

I found them deep in my junk drawer:
5" blades (cutting edge, inner blade,
hollow). Stainless, silver, sharp, still as a moth.

The finger rest and the finger ring: wings
pivoting on the steel heart of a fat screw.
My friend once asked me: *don't you think scissors*

kind of look like angels? if you open them?
Outside, the extra ashy Lenten light: crucifixions
in the sky, flying things. Perhaps I'll cut and steal

forsythia branches hanging over my backyard fence.
Here are the roots of scissors: *the leaves*
of a plant; the tooth of a comb; the cut and the strike.

On the news, five men and a woman
tried to predict the future, flitted around some point.
Time severed, landed inside my back porch light.

At the Corner of Assunta and Camille Roads, Revere, Massachusetts

I didn't expect the majority of the
Italian-American community . . .
to abandon me by their silence,
Geraldine Ferraro

A small gray pregnant cat was lifted
by the talons of a hawk: the brown and white bird

carried its prey past the over-grown blue fir
and the afternoon moon, which loomed like Mary's breast

pressed against the sky-window. As the cat flew,
she watched the low-pitched roofs

of the new ranches, the dug-out foundations—homes
she would never live in. The moon

surrendered itself to this tableau:
the gray cat, the hawk that had never been seen

before in this neighborhood, all the hunger.
Weeks earlier, some boys caught that gold and black snake

dangling deep within the blue fir's branches.
She would visit from the dug-up pond

where houses would go. They chased her until
she wore out from reticulation: her long spine

unable to move quick like brain waves in a dream.
I can barely write this: the boys looped her into a brown

lunch bag, doused it with gas, lit it on fire. The cat did not
see this and the hawk, alighting by the muddy pond,

released her. She stepped from under its wing,
uncertain. I still don't know if this was a dream or

a memory—the cat, the black and gold snake.
There was charred skin, there were tire strips, there was

a laboring cat. The whole neighborhood, nascent, silent.

Self-Portrait as the Half-Dead Cherry Tree
Outside the Bedroom Window

I've re-taken my daughter's room,
gone back to the time before children,
when I wore an 18-karat rope chain around

my neck to my breastbone and dangled
a gold-plated razor blade, an Italian horn,
a miraculous medal for lost causes, a vial.

What happened is this: I wanted the impossible:
for you, ignorant of my indifference, to love me.
Do you understand this greed? As a child,

my dolls were hybrids: part dog, part cowgirl,
a small devil. I found my father's baby doll
at my grandma's, in her back bedroom

off the kitchen with the Befana witch. The doll's
porcelain skull shattered over its fontanel. Grandma said
not to tell anyone ever about this thing I'd found.

How do we survive sadness?
Like a dream, is my sadness only interesting to me?

Last year, the cherry tree blossomed for the first time
in a long while. It had been split and split again by bolts
of lightning that cracked the road as well.

Vanquished

. . . do you think . . . that the Soviets might be
tempted to try to take advantage of you simply
because you are a woman? Robert Boyd, 1984

At MoMA, I stood too close to a Joseph Cornell box,

Taglioni's Jewel Casket. I'd been thinking of buying

a yard of plush velvet to stretch taut across a canvas,

of pinning or gluing loose pearls to the dark mossy surface.

Taglioni's story captured Cornell: that late-night moment

when she danced for the Russian robber, a highwayman,

on a panther's pelt thrown over the snow

and each muscled grunt froze in the Eurasian air,

crystalized before she landed her perfect jeté.

She carried a glass cube after that to remember how

she vanquished him. I wanted to create my own night sky,

a collage of stars, constellations: The Queen, The Coke-Whore,

The Madonna, The Constellation of Return. I'd add a dark blue

sky wheel to mark seasons. I'd pin everything I lost, try to capture what I love or loved, even deep midnight sadness. Cornell's box,

that jewel casket, held: glass cubes for Taglioni, a cheap rhinestone

choker from Woolworth's for the stars, a brown velvet lining

for the pelt, a small pane of blue glass to dance upon.

Honeymoon During the Reagan Administration

Three martello towers stood round and abandoned on a dried field within the walls of Old Quebec City. There were no wars anymore, no need for garrisons, no need to hide men. (My new name meant hammer, too, or little hammer: his sister wanted me to share a surname with her, or she felt this was important, after a night of cocaine, when everything was manic and important.) Later, at the Argentinian steakhouse, below the sidewalk, where the walls were brick and cool, he and I ate raw meat and potato shoestrings. I wore chunky necklaces: fat, fake rubies, glass emeralds and topaz. My poor body was sore. (The clitoris, aroused and exposed, was described once as a tower or hill made of red mud and spit housing termites.) The cold ground had seeped through my cracked Doc Martens, made my legs ache in tight jeans—you'd think we did it right there, on the field, on my military coat (the one with shoulder pads like a tin soldier).

Rhymes, Slant and Otherwise

. . . I can't say it but it rhymes with rich,
Barbara Bush, 1984, regarding Geraldine
Ferraro

A patch in a field of hairy purple vetch?

                A round oak table for an oily klatch?

A Cuban cigar and a burnt-out match?

                Amazing grace saving not one wretch?

A Dutch Elm leaf-clogged drainage ditch?

                An oxblood Ivy League skull & bones
                watch?

Mid-month full pearl moon and the silhouette of a witch on a broom?

                A tombstone-country with a rusted
                crotch and sturdy latch?

An avocado and burnt umber kitchen full of kitsch?

                Noxzema in a cobalt jar for your son's
                sunburn itch?

A thick glass of smoky oaken bourbon down the long, final hatch? .

Rue

And then I realized the coronavirus was a woman

who's been ignored for too long, and now

she holds sway, she lumbers like

the Elephant Queen, the big tusker,

the last of her kind, determined to end

wherever she wants.

No one dares

bump into this woman. She puts on her red

pearl crown and everybody—are you

happy now—has to watch her, listen

to what she has to say.

I told my friends this today,

some virtually, some six feet away. I told them this

through the dry and cold ides of March air and,

maybe because they love me, no one looked surprised.

Watching Clips of the Democratic National Convention, July 19, 1984

There she was, looking beautiful and looking female, Cokie Roberts

Pearls encircle Geraldine Ferraro like tiny moons around a mother earth. Pearls

    created from mother of pearl, protective: that iridescent layer, the hard

        luminescent surface inside the hinged shell.

Ferraro wears long strands, long to her breast bone. Back then, I took fistfuls

    of tiny fake strings—white, gold, gray—and I'd twist them like cables,

        wore them tight and torqued around my neck.

As I watch the clips of the nomination of Geraldine Ferraro to the Vice Presidency

    of the United States, I look away, out my east-facing window

        to the warm sun, warm finally this late in June. The doomed

Japanese cherry tree, split, then split again by lightning bolts, flowered
   for the first time

   this season, flowered pink and full of tiny leaves so lush and

      tangled, I almost forget the thick branches we lost to the
      chainsaw.

My name, she says, *is Geraldine Ferraro*. All the women reach their
arms up to her,

   wave and reach as if offered open-handed a merciful pearl,

      a grace, one time, then snatched back and slapped shut.

Pearls

In the end, those months
just before the final purple twilight, my mother

would look around the nursing home
realizing what was happening. She didn't

realize Joanie and I were already cleaning out the house.
In the other bedroom we found Liz's cans of Aqua Net—

long sprayed out—a Louis Vuitton clutch—
a real one—we found a fake

strand of pearls—too fat and light
to be made of real spit. They lay

coiled in a black velvet case that snapped
shut on the skin between my thumb and pointer.

Do you want these? Would you wear them? No one
wore pearls anymore. My mother would cry

so loud and hard, the nurse, afraid
she'd upset the other women on the floor,

let her sit at the front desk,
shuffle through old *Time*

magazines, receipts, as if she worked there,
as if she still had tasks to complete.

The Angels of Hanover Street

and she let him control her limbs
and her body, Mario Puzo

I'm finishing a late supper with Laurette and Julia and Diana at Riccardo's next to the Italian-American bookstore in Boston's North End. The white table cloth is stained with circles: purple wine, gold olive oil, and black coffee. Laurette says she will never watch or read *The Godfather*. I tell them the first time I snuck that book into my bed and read the sex scene, I thought Sonny Corleone broke the hipbones of Lucy Mancini. When I read "blood-gorged pole of muscle," I thought he was bleeding; when I read "shattering climax," I thought pieces of her bones splattered across her silk maid-of-honor gown. I didn't know how things in a woman really could be broken. The doctor who tightened Lucy *down there* with loops of surgical thread so she could constrict around him, called her *poor benighted Eye-talian girl*. I say, *Well, maybe* The Godfather *is an inkblot test for Italians.* In the book, Don Corleone said, *Women and children can afford to be careless, men cannot.* I love it here, in the oldest part of the city: the sticky sweet streets, the lights lit all year, the little girl-tinsel-angels dangling from hooks.

Aunt Olga Argenzio

Her brother gave her the attic to live in and a hot plate. The branches from the silver blue pine out back grew high enough to scratch the walls: something made house there. She kept her old doll on the twin bed and a box of pop-a-beads on a small bureau by the gable window. I would make necklaces over and over by sticking the plastic knobbed end into the hole of the other bead just for the satisfaction of pulling them apart, for the pop of air sucking out. When I grew older, I remembered this and how it was like sex and how it was like time. All the beads were olives: green, brown, black. She had to bathe in her brother's apartment on the second floor: Uncle G. wouldn't pay for plumbing her room. Once, when I was a child, I ran up from his sister's—my grandma's—apartment on the first floor where everybody ate, ran through the cool back hallway where the wine hung in baskets and the belts and my grandpa's old fireman's jacket—ran up to see my uncle who sat alone and migrained in his dark parlor. He sat below an oil painting of a woman clinging to a stone cross in grief or in gratitude: the cross had no savior, though, just a gray eye, watching me. When I was old enough to articulate the questions, I asked my mother if I had dreamed this. She didn't look up from her ironing (all my father's white shirts)—*no, that probably happened.* Aunt Olga, years before she died, would come to our house, the new ranch, to iron those shirts, but we couldn't tell anyone that she did this. She told her boyfriend—an Irishman from Brighton—that she didn't believe women should be ordained. I remember, over a plate of golden calamari rings, how she said how wrong it was to even ask this. In 1984, when the cancer found her fast, I got lost in the hospital searching for her death room. Wigless, she lay like an old man finally: bald, dull silver, her nose what they call Roman: hawk-like, her mouth moving, thirsty, prayer-less.

Madonna, Triptych, 1984

My heart beat boom boom boom
when I stole things from my parents' room:

tortoiseshell cup, the rosaries I grabbed in my fist—
some tarnished, one with a bone crucifix.

On the bureau, the triptych mirror refracted light
from the windows with ivory drapes and blinds.

The stone Madonna wore my favorite strand:
the pearl rosary moons on a tarnished chain.

I held five decades of luminescent spit
and mother of pearl to my breast, my lips,

fingered the beads, all sweaty and tangled—
my ribcage felt corseted laced up and bridled.

No one ever missed a single thing
or heard me leave—I think

*

even in my dreams I feared no one
would ever hear me. Last night I tugged

a steel knife from an old wound, diseased—
the long cool blade pulled easily

from a cloudy sky: the sky at night
refracting the pearl milk moon full and fat.

On my pine bureau, the tortoiseshell cup
holds the pearl and blonde wood beads, dust

clogs their chains, dust sprinkles down
like starlight through the open windows,

and because this is my dream, the knife
becomes a black and silver corded mic

I hold to my breast, my lips.
The long cord wrapped around me, my ribs—

*

and because this is my dream, the mic
belongs to Madonna crawling in white

across the dusty stage in tulle and lace,
corseted, a bride like a virgin, her necklaces—

three strands of pearls, rhinestones for refraction.
A fat rosary with globe decades tightened

around her neck: the choker gleams,
echoes her silver boytoy belt, and still she

sings, *oooh you make me feel ooooh*
yeah you make me feel shiny and new—

all laced up in whale bone or plastic stays
ribcaged Madonna gets down girl-cow low,

drags that crucifix across the wood. It looms
over the waxy shine, bounces to the bass beat boom.

When Was My Anger Conceived?

The summer of assassinations?

By the man-made lake? A hole
so shallow and muddy, all the men
held hands, formed a human net and
walked toward each other to the center
to feel for some kid who might have
gone under—there,

on its shore, in the Kodak, me,
in my little terry cloth bikini,
all round as the moon stomach.
I'd worn a Batman mask attached

by a thin rubber band all summer,
my hands fisted, the nails bit crescents
in my palms.

The summer of my menarche?

Against the lazy Susan in the kitchen I stood,
watching the President resign on the small TV:
I cried because of the cramps and blood,
the garter belt biting me. My mother said
we'd never see this again and she was wrong:

even married to my father,
she couldn't predict the depth
of a man's rage.

The summer of my first abortion?

The clinic three stops down
from my dorm, three quick stops
on the Green Line, and no one shot
there yet but escorts needed, one pink
set of rosaries flung at my face.

That year, 1984, my aunt said she wouldn't vote
for anything that menstruated, could get pregnant,
could bear a child.

Succulent

I want to fill a bay window with sixteen jade plants
in terra cotta pots until they grow thick and knotted as snakes

tangling in the hair of a woman raped by a god
and punished by a woman.

I want to tease rubbery pearl beads of *asterids* into a rosary string,
finger them, pray on them, try not to let the toxin seep onto my skin.

I want to snap off a fat oozy leaf of the aloe I kept
in the middle of my blue table: rub the silm on my scalded hands—

I want to grow the round black and shiny *phytolacca* on a high
shelf, away from Maria, my long-hair cat, hide them

from pregnant women who want to keep their babies
from bleeding out. I always seem to want too much.

I want my succulents to survive me. They can live
for a long time without water, without touch.

Write a Poem About the Number 16

It is easier to split a heap of grain into 16 equal parts than into 10.

Pantone makes one (16-15) shade of white.

16 luminescent pearls or more to compliment a white dress.

When Geraldine Ferraro was seated in the 96th Congress of the United
States,

    there were 16 women in the House of Representatives.

16 women taking a man's seat.

435 seats less 419 seats saved for men = 16 seats left.

16 x 2 = number of years to lift the blood ban on men who have sex
with men.

16 is the youngest one can be to donate blood.

16, the cruelest age for women or the sweetest: in some states,
the age of consent.

Only when Walter Mondale ran 16 polling points behind
Ronald Reagan in 1983,

    did he choose a woman as his running mate.

In 1983, *Metis*, composed of ice and water, the 16th moon of Jupiter, was named for the Titaness of Wisdom and Prudence.

In (16 x 2) – 11 years, another woman again and even I laughed at her.

White for the next acceptance speech (16 x 2 years) in 2000 + 16.

16 + 40 years of my waiting.

16 x X = 0, solve for X.

Yesterday, I Was So Angry, I Broke Things With My Mind

The chunky juice glass on the granite counter. The cat's chipped

saucers for kibble and cream. The thick white mug, its shattered curves

     lay in fat white pieces, thick as oyster shells, the brokenness

     capturing light like a poem about the moon or the moon's

memory of tide. I've been angry for so long. Or maybe just afraid

of not really being here: parts of me in pieces—left eye,

     my upper lip, the third rib, the mound at the base of my thumb.

     One of those seasonal constellations connected with a finger.

Cleaning it up was hardest: its skinny pieces reflected

blue and cold, hungry, like a mirror. They wanted the tender

     instep, the callused sole. They wanted the deep green-purple

     vein. I swept and swept with my favorite whisk broom but

still, the tiny slivers shone all over my floor, a night sky

magnetic and inversed.

Root

I bought a new knife, sliced an onion through its skin,
through its sixteen layers. I was Sylvian and Plathian.
I sliced close to the nail bed of my left ring finger,

low to the lunula. This is my winter of hangnails
and split nails. I spit nails: crescent moons
fly out of my mouth and across the maple wood floor and

little white knives of cartilage sprout still hinged
to my skin, catch on my gray wool wrap. The root
of anger is the kissing cousin of hangnail. Today

I learned that pearls without cores make the ideal
sculpting medium if you were to sculpt skulls—
the skins don't crack or peel. I can never wed again.

The kissing cousin of anger is angina: a stab wound
to my sacred heart, the one wound with wire. My grandma
said if we swallowed seeds from a fruit we'd grow

that tree in our stomachs; if we swallowed
the fingernails we chewed off, our tummies
would be torn open by the claws we grew.

And Yet, And Yet

"What About 'The Breakfast Club'? Revisiting
the Movies of My Youth in the Age of
#MeToo," Molly Ringwald

at the end of the movie, Molly folded her left diamond stud

into Judd's fingerless-gloved fist which he pumped high,

triumphant, frozen in that '80s stop action, rewarded after a day

at Shermer High School, Shermer, Illinois, in 1984, for his slow

clap after her perfect cleavage lipstick rub (how ashamed

she was, dragging the color from her own full lips), after calling her

Queenie for hours, after crawling through the tunnel her legs made

below the desk where he ducked (and I could feel it, his long dirty hair

tickling the insides of her thighs): I remember loving that suede sarong

(I mean, to own such a thing in high school) and how she matched

her outfit perfectly: the pink V-neck shirt with that rich brown pelt.

Nancy Pelosi's Beads, 1984–Present

She wore *Eye of the Tiger, Thrill of the Fight* orange striped beads: they
shone—

her tiger eyes shone, even in the photos, they shone like a wet pelt.

Tahitian South Sea Pearls: *spectacular, emotional, thunderous:*

sky blue and gold, sky blue and gold, sky blue and gold, sky blue and
gold, clasped.

How we see the past from the future: gold snake eggs in an owl's beak.

In the '80s we all looked like little men with big shoulder pads.

Pelosi's beads so dark they reflected how endless and orbital.

I like a story that turns on itself like a wounded animal:

a story that curves the way a spine curves, licks itself clean, scented,
whole.

Careless folk confused her mace with a caduceus: she's not here to heal.

The mace she pinned to her breast held a pearl atop 13 bound gold rods.

Pelosi's jade beads, Easter egg yellow beads, chaste beads, torqued
her throat.

Her Mariquita Masterson beads: blue-black gumballs to choke a horse—
she wore them around her neck like war trophies clasped with two
thick red hooks.

The Year of Geraldine Ferraro Duplex

You can't make a man look that bad and live.
When I got sober, I was told to forgive.

But how do I stay sober after I forgive?
A brutal man gave me a gray pearl ring—

Broke his brutal teeth on my gray pearl ring.
He wanted to eat me up so I'd disappear.

He thought he'd eaten me all, but no, I didn't disappear.
I sat in his boozy belly, all warm red and pink.

Warm in my belly, my booze all sweet and pink.
Would you rather feel anger than sadness?

Would you rather feel angrily all of your sadnesses?
How sweet must you be to be loved by God?

How sweet is the silence in the belly of God?
You can't make that man look bad and live.

I Don't Have It, Do You?

—Larry Speakes, Deputy Press Secretary to
Ronald Reagan, October 15, 1982

Lentivirus: long incubation. *Lent*: long days. *Lent*: it shall be
returned.

I stay awake until first pearl light.

The whole world has been cancelled and so there is no time.

I remember that man who joked about death and then he died
from Alzheimer's.

My mother also died from Alzheimer's and so there is no God.

Deep into coronavirus's sway, I drove through the rain to my
childhood home.

That man joked for three years: joked about fairies and kissing:
things he believed made a man less of a man, things he believed
made a man a woman.

My mother forgot everything but her fear and so there is no justice.

The new owners put a stone façade over part of the old house: tonal
colors my mother would have liked. Big blocks of fake rock.

The Challenger

January 28, 1986

I came home to my mother and cried myself into strep
fevering over a boy who wouldn't answer me,

       wouldn't stay or

maybe I was sweating Absolut vodka out through my skin.
She was folding my father's shirts (later she would fold washcloths

over and over and I married that boy). Neither of us
could read stars or runes or bones or crystal balls or entrails—

It was a clear blue day and so cold no cloud
could form, no bird in the air:

        they'd flown south

I suppose they migrated or they died. I could see the sky
from the basement windows, see the blue coming through

reflecting off the wood paneling and the gold linoleum.
We watched the clear warm Florida sky on the big

television (in the cabinet with the stereo and its
linty needle). The rocket carrying the teacher climbed.

smoke billowing white clouds, the only clouds on the east-
ern seaboard it seemed and then:

the intestines of a white

god spread. I wondered *is that supposed to happen high
up?* I wondered if my boyfriend would call. If I could

get more coke. So high—48,000 feet above the Atlantic—
the rocket curved at its apex and began its fall, returned home.

Two years into his second term, The President
assured us all that *the future doesn't belong*

to the fainthearted . . . it belongs to the brave.
I will meet it with joy. Maybe he didn't know, couldn't tell us

they were alive   in that ship   alive for the slow arcing high
in the blue sky   alive   for the long descent

to the ocean rushing

up to meet them.

Forgetting

I am unbaked bread because I'm soft and I rise
on a wooden kneading board carved in the shape of a pig.
Inside my yeasty gut, a small pearl of old-country dough
implants in the pink lining, a starter pearl grown so long ago,
some people call it *mother.*

I am a monolingual orphan ashamed of my tongue,
ashamed of my ancient language, its reversed syntax,
its thick jeweled vowels.

I am the gap between those strong teeth that stayed rooted
in my grandma's mouth while she lay dying
in the dark wood twin-sized bed next to grandpa's.
In between that gap, on a night table, a dried-out palm
and a dark pearl rosary wound around the green cut-glass lamp.

I am the conversation about golden Boscs
and mortadella with its pearls of fat—
how I hate the grainy meat of a pear
and that salty cock-shape hanging trussed in the deli window.
I am that hate, too.

Someday, I won't be late to things. Or I will be late.

Or I won't care.

I am the bone buttons on a gray cardigan: I am the tongue
and teeth that bite the buttons right off the wool.

I am the crown of one Neapolitan cypress too shy
to touch the crown of the other.

After the period at the end of a staccato
sentence, I am the long breath through the lips,
the double space no one here uses anymore.

NOTES

When I began writing the poems that would become *The Queen of Queens*, I was really just memorializing the early '80s. 1984 was my second presidential election, and the first time I would be casting a vote for a woman, Geraldine Ferraro, to the executive branch. This was during the Reagan Administration's chilling indifference to the AIDS epidemic. I couldn't foresee the COVID-19 pandemic and the Trump Administration's fatal mishandling. I couldn't foresee the wonderful and historic election of our first woman Vice President, Kamala Harris. The circularity of events is chilling and, at the same time, fitting.

Most of the quotations used as epigraphs and within the poems come from the following sources:

Geraldine A. Ferraro (with Linda Bird Francke), *Ferraro, My Story* (Evanston: Northwestern University Press, 1985).

Joan Quigley, *"What Does Joan Say?" My Seven Years as White House Astrologer to Nancy and Ronald Reagan* (New York: Carol Publishing Group, 1990).

Some of the poems were inspired by the following interviews and articles:

"Journal Takes the Low Road," Mike Barnicle, *The Boston Globe*, September 24, 1984.

"Whaddah ya mean accent? She Talks Queens!" Maureen Dowd, *The New York Times*, October 1, 1984.

"What About the Breakfast Club: Revisiting the Movies of My Youth in the age of #MeToo," Molly Ringwald, *The New Yorker*, April 6, 2018.

And the documentaries:

Geraldine Ferraro: Paving the Way. Donna Zaccaro (director), October 11, 2013, http://www.ferraropavingtheway.com

When AIDS Was Funny. Scott Calonico (director), 2015, https://www.youtube.com/watch?v=yAzDn7tE1lU

"The proud boast of the Empire State, the first lady of the Big Apple, the Queen of Queens," Mario Cuomo introduced Geraldine Ferraro on August 1, 1984 in Queens, New York.

"from *Jezebel*: "Map: Six Decades of the Most Popular Name for Girls, State by State," https://jezebel.com/map-sixty-years-of-the-most-popular-names-for-girls-s-1443501909.

"The Star Sign of the Moscone Center, July 19, 1984," "I wanna be the one to walk in the sun," is from Cyndi Lauper's "Girls Just Want to Have Fun," (*She's So Unusual*, 1983).

"My Father Was an Italian Man. So Are My Husband and My Son." The title of this American sonnet is a quote from Geraldine Ferraro, 1984.

"He is My Man.   He is My Tomato." Geraldine Ferraro was misquoted as saying this ridiculous sentence. "A Washington reporter, who interviewed the candidate last week on her campaign plane about the difficult times that her husband, John A. Zaccaro, has been through, reported that she stood by him, saying, 'He is my man, he is my tomato.' Aides had no explanation for the divergence. "She was probably asking the stewardess for a mayonnaise and tomato sandwich," joked Beth Sheridan, an assistant press secretary." (NYT, October 1, 1984).

"Toxic Shock Duplex" and "The Year of Geraldine Ferraro Duplex" both use a poetic form, the duplex, invented by Jericho Brown. "Year of Geraldine Ferraro Duplex" begins with a quote by Ferraro after her debate with George H.W. Bush, October 11, 1984. In 1980, Proctor and Gamble removed superabsorbent tampons (Rely) which "blossomed" when inserted. Doctors determined these caused a spike in toxic shock syndrome cases.

"Cisoria," *the terrible wind tries its breathing*, is a line from Roberto Calasso's *The Marriage of Cadmus and Harmony*. Vintage, February 8, 1994.

"Rhymes, Slant and Otherwise," Barbara Bush, when asked what she thought about Geraldine Ferraro following the vice presidential debate, responded with, "That four million dollar . . . I can't say it but it rhymes with rich." Mrs. Bush immediately regretted this and called Congresswoman Ferraro to apologize.

"*Write a Poem About the Number 16*" references the FDA ban on accepting blood donations from men who have had sex with men. The ban was implemented in 1983 and lifted in 2015 (32 years).

"Root," The word "anger" has a strange root: it is etymologically related to "angina" and "hangnail." *The New York Times*, November 24, 2019

"*Vice Presidential Acceptance Speech, by Congresswoman Geraldine Ferraro, July 19, 1984*," When I began this erasure, Kamala Harris was not Vice President. After her glorious election victory, I encased and crossed out the "not"—a double erasure!

"The Challenger" uses a line from President Ronald Reagan's remarks after The Challenger explosion, https://history.nasa.gov/reagan12886.html. There has also been speculation that the crew did not die immediately.

"Forgetting" is for Louise DeSalvo (b. September 27, 1942, d. October 31, 2018).

ACKNOWLEDGMENTS

Arcturus, Chicago Review of Books "Mal'Occhio"

Broadsided Press "Cisoria"

First Literary Review Journal-East "Fugue"

Ghost Bible "Toxic Shock Duplex"

Heavy Feather Review "Relinquishing," "*He Was My Man, He Was My Tomato*"

Italian Americana Cultural and Historical Review "Vanquished"

Luna Luna "Tongue Root," "16 Reasons I Became a Gray Pearl"

Muddy River Poetry Review "*Shout, Shout,*" "Nancy Pelosi's Beads, 1984-present," "*I Sleep in the Daytime,*" "*And Yet, And Yet*"

The New Verse News "Questions to the Electorate"

On the Seawall "Watching Clips of the Democratic National Convention, July 19, 1984," "Oracular," "In the Year of Ferraro"

Ovunque Siamo, New Italian-American Writing "Aunt Olga Argenzio," "Forgetting," "Strega"

Painted Bride Quarterly "Succulent"

Paterson Literary Review "Yesterday, I Was So Angry, I Broke Things With My Mind," "Pearls"

Pine Hills Review "from *Jezebel*: "Map: Six Decades of the Most Popular Name for Girls, State by State"

Pithead Chapel "Prognostication"

Solstice: A Magazine of Diverse Voices "*My Father Was an Italian Man. So Are My Husband and My Son,*" (published as "Sometimes When My Stiff Joints Pop, Women Appear and Want to Talk to Me.")

South Florida Poetry Journal "Self-Portrait as the Half-Dead Cherry Tree Outside the Bedroom Window"

Sweet: A Literary Confection "Root"

3 Elements Literary Review "Honeymoon During the Reagan Era"

West Trestle Review "Grey Figs and Leaves, by Wedgwood"

What Rough Beast (Indolent Books) *"I Don't Have It, Do You?"*

White Stag Journal "Agrodolce"

The following poems appeared in the chapbook, *In the Year of Ferraro*, from Nixes Mate Books:

"The Star Sign of the Moscone Center, July 19, 1984," "Why I Began Writing About Vice-Presidential Candidate, Geraldine Ferraro," "When Was My Anger Conceived?" "At the Corner of Assunta and Camille Roads, Revere, Massachusetts," "The Year of Geraldine Ferraro Duplex," "Rhymes, Slant and Otherwise (originally, "Barbara Bush's Thoughts on Geraldine Ferraro,"), *"Write a Poem About the Number 16,"* "The Challenger"

"Cisoria" also appeared in anthology, *Voices Amidst the Virus: Poets Respond to the Pandemic,* Lily Poetry Review

"Madonna Triptych," appeared in the anthology, *Mother Mary Comes to Me: A Pop Culture Poetry Anthology,* Madville Publishing

"Honeymoon During the Reagan Administration" also appeared in *The Uncanny Valley,* Big Table Publishers.

"Rue" appeared in the anthology, *Oxygen: Parables of Pandemic,* River Paw Press.

Thank you to the following people:

My beloved friends taken needlessly and too soon by AIDS.

Nicholas Grosso at Bordighera Press who has been such a support for my work.

Michael McInnis at Nixes Mate Books for publishing *In the Year of Ferraro* as part of the Fly Cotton Chapbook Series; for seeing Ferraro as part of history.

The Italian American Writers Association and I AM Books in Boston for giving us all a place to be. Thank you to all the literati who returned month after month to support each other's voices!

Julia Lisella, Maria Lisella, Laurette Viteritti-Folk, Olivia Kate Cerrone, and Diana Lynch for sisterhood.

Jennifer Jean, January Gill O'Neil, Cindy Veach, Carla Panciera, Danielle Jones, Rebecca Kinzie Bastian, Kali Lightfoot, Kathleen Aguero, Richard Hoffman, Dawn Paul, Colleen Michaels, M.P. Carver, Clay Ventre, J.D. Scrimgeour, Kevin Carey, Michelle Messina Reale, and Chad Frame for everything.

Vin, Mia, and Michael Martelli. Joan Colella Bullock and Liz Colella Kirk. My family. I love you.

Shirley Chisholm, Geraldine Ferraro, Hillary Clinton, and Kamala Devi Harris, for all you've manifested.

ABOUT THE AUTHOR

JENNIFER MARTELLI is the author of *My Tarantella* (Bordighera Press), awarded an Honorable Mention from the Italian-American Studies Association, selected as a "Must Read" by the Massachusetts Center for the Book, and named as a finalist for the Housatonic Book Award. She is also the author of the chapbooks *In the Year of Ferraro* from Nixes Mate Press and *After Bird*, winner of the Grey Book Press open reading, 2016. Her work has appeared in The Academy of American Poets *Poem-a-Day*, *The Tahoma Literary Review*, *Thrush*, *The Sycamore Review*, *Cream City Review*, *Verse Daily*, *Iron Horse Review* (winner of the Photo Finish contest), *Poetry*, and elsewhere. Jennifer Martelli has twice received grants from the Massachusetts Cultural Council for her poetry.

NICOLE SANTALUCIA. *Because I Did Not Die.* Vol 115. Poetry.

MARK CIABATTARI. *Preludes to History.* Vol 114. Poetry.

HELEN BAROLINI. *Visits.* Vol 113. Novel.

ERNESTO LIVORNI. *The Fathers' America.* Vol 112. Poetry.

MARIO B. MIGNONE. *The Story of My People.* Vol 111. Non-fiction.

GEORGE GUIDA. *The Sleeping Gulf.* Vol 110. Poetry.

JOEY NICOLETTI. *Reverse Graffiti.* Vol 109. Poetry.

GIOSE RIMANELLI. *Il mestiere del furbo.* Vol 108. Criticism.

LEWIS TURCO. *The Hero Enkidu.* Vol 107. Poetry.

AL TACCONELLI. *Perhaps Fly.* Vol 106. Poetry.

RACHEL GUIDO DEVRIES. *A Woman Unknown in Her Bones.* Vol 105. Poetry.

BERNARD BRUNO. *A Tear and a Tear in My Heart.* Vol 104. Non-fiction.

FELIX STEFANILE. *Songs of the Sparrow.* Vol 103. Poetry.

FRANK POLIZZI. *A New Life with Bianca.* Vol 102. Poetry.

GIL FAGIANI. *Stone Walls.* Vol 101. Poetry.

LOUISE DESALVO. *Casting Off.* Vol 100. Fiction.

MARY JO BONA. *I Stop Waiting for You.* Vol 99. Poetry.

RACHEL GUIDO DEVRIES. *Stati zitt, Josie.* Vol 98. Children's Literature. $8

GRACE CAVALIERI. *The Mandate of Heaven.* Vol 97. Poetry.

MARISA FRASCA. *Via incanto.* Vol 96. Poetry.

DOUGLAS GLADSTONE. *Carving a Niche for Himself.* Vol 95. History.

MARIA TERRONE. *Eye to Eye.* Vol 94. Poetry.

CONSTANCE SANCETTA. *Here in Cerchio.* Vol 93. Local History.

MARIA MAZZIOTTI GILLAN. *Ancestors' Song.* Vol 92. Poetry.

MICHAEL PARENTI. *Waiting for Yesterday: Pages from a Street Kid's Life.* Vol 90. Memoir.

ANNIE LANZILLOTTO. *Schistsong.* Vol 89. Poetry.

EMANUEL DI PASQUALE. *Love Lines.* Vol 88. Poetry.

CAROSONE & LOGIUDICE. *Our Naked Lives.* Vol 87. Essays.

JAMES PERICONI. *Strangers in a Strange Land: A Survey of Italian-Language American Books.* Vol 86. Book History.

DANIELA GIOSEFFI. *Escaping La Vita Della Cucina.* Vol 85. Essays.

MARIA FAMÀ. *Mystics in the Family.* Vol 84. Poetry.

ROSSANA DEL ZIO. *From Bread and Tomatoes to Zuppa di Pesce "Ciambotto".* Vol. 83. Memoir.

LORENZO DELBOCA. *Polentoni.* Vol 82. Italian Studies.

SAMUEL GHELLI. *A Reference Grammar.* Vol 81. Italian Language.

ROSS TALARICO. *Sled Run.* Vol 80. Fiction.

FRED MISURELLA. *Only Sons.* Vol 79. Fiction.

FRANK LENTRICCHIA. *The Portable Lentricchia.* Vol 78. Fiction.

RICHARD VETERE. *The Other Colors in a Snow Storm.* Vol 77. Poetry.

GARIBALDI LAPOLLA. *Fire in the Flesh.* Vol 76 Fiction & Criticism.

GEORGE GUIDA. *The Pope Stories.* Vol 75 Prose.

ROBERT VISCUSI. *Ellis Island.* Vol 74. Poetry.

ELENA GIANINI BELOTTI. *The Bitter Taste of Strangers Bread.* Vol 73. Fiction.

PINO APRILE. *Terroni.* Vol 72. Italian Studies.

CPSIA information can be obtained
at www.ICGtesting.com
Printed in the USA
BVHW071925010422
632801BV00002B/128